THIS TODDLER COLORING BOOK BELONGS TO

Apple
A

Banana

Coconut

D
Dragon

E
Elderberry

Feijoa

G
Guava

Huckleberry

I ce
Cream

Jujuba
J

K

Kiwi

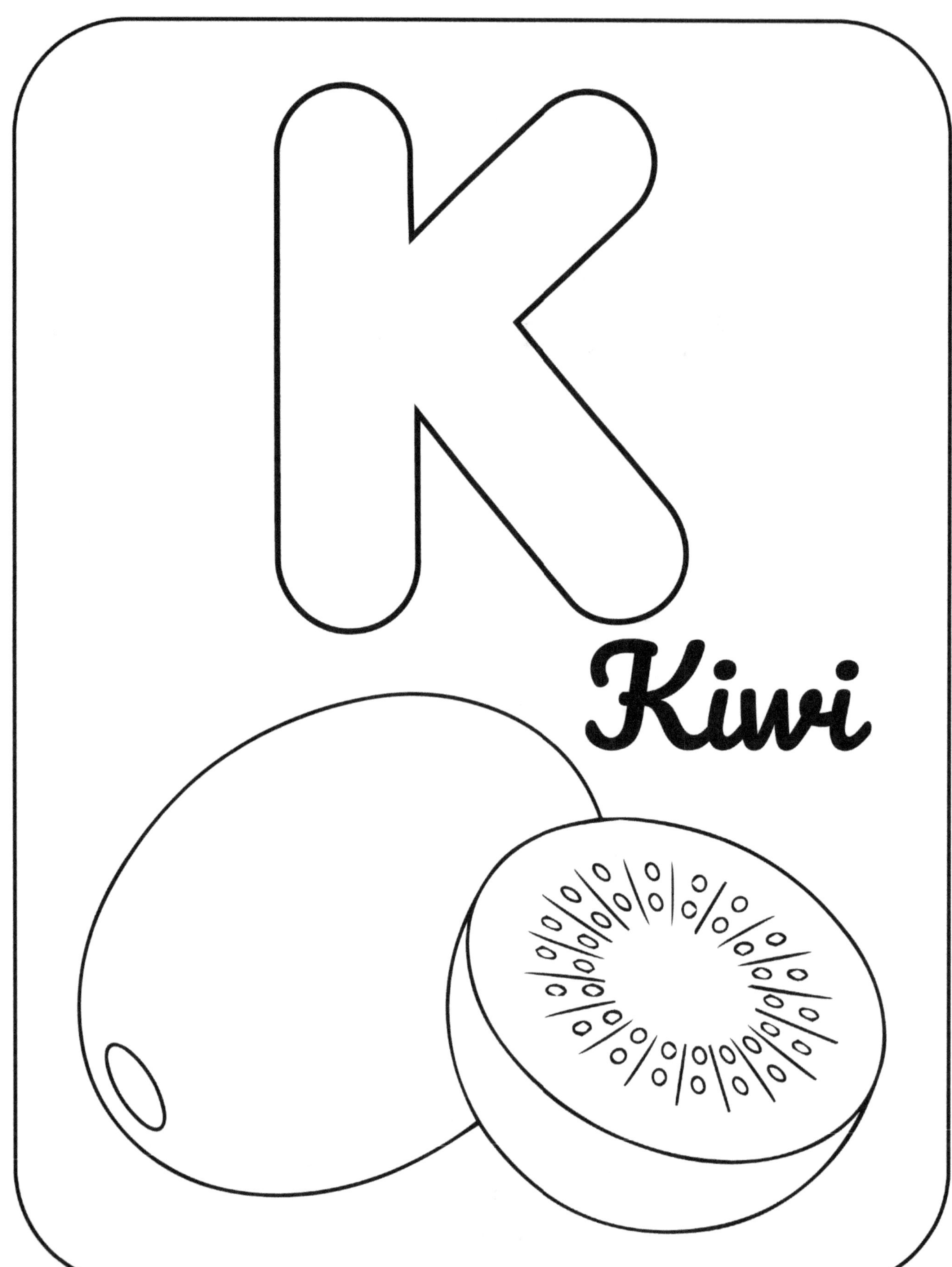

Lemon

M

Mango

N

Nectarine

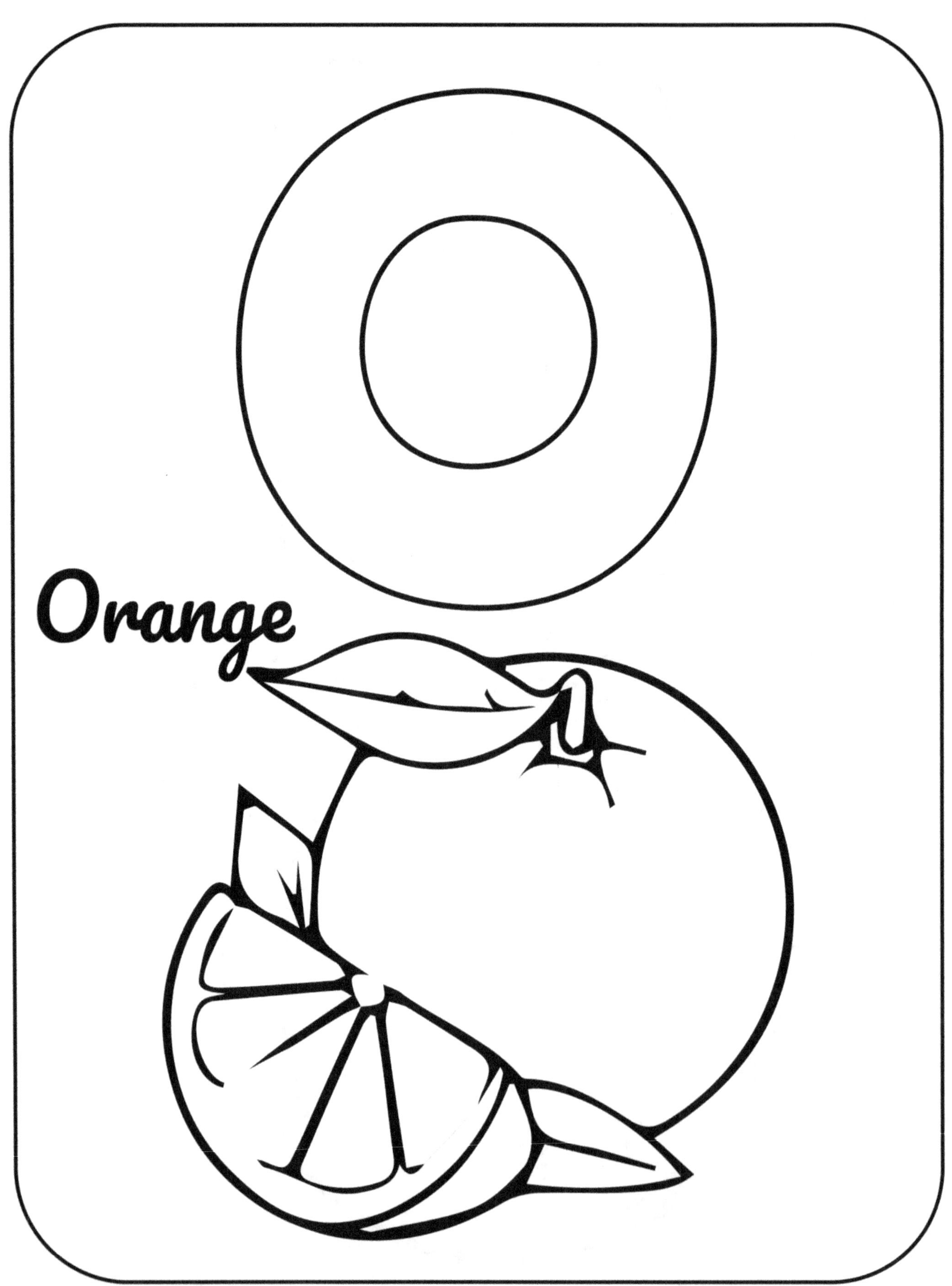
Orange

P
Pineapple

Q

Quince

R

Radish

S
Strawberry

T
Tomato

Ugly Fruit

V

Vidalia Onions

W
Watermelon

Ximenia

Y
Yam

Z

Zucchini

1 2 3 4
5 6 7 8
9 10
NUMBER

1

ONE

TWO

3

THREE

FOUR

5
FIVE

6
SIX

SEVEN

EIGHT

NINE

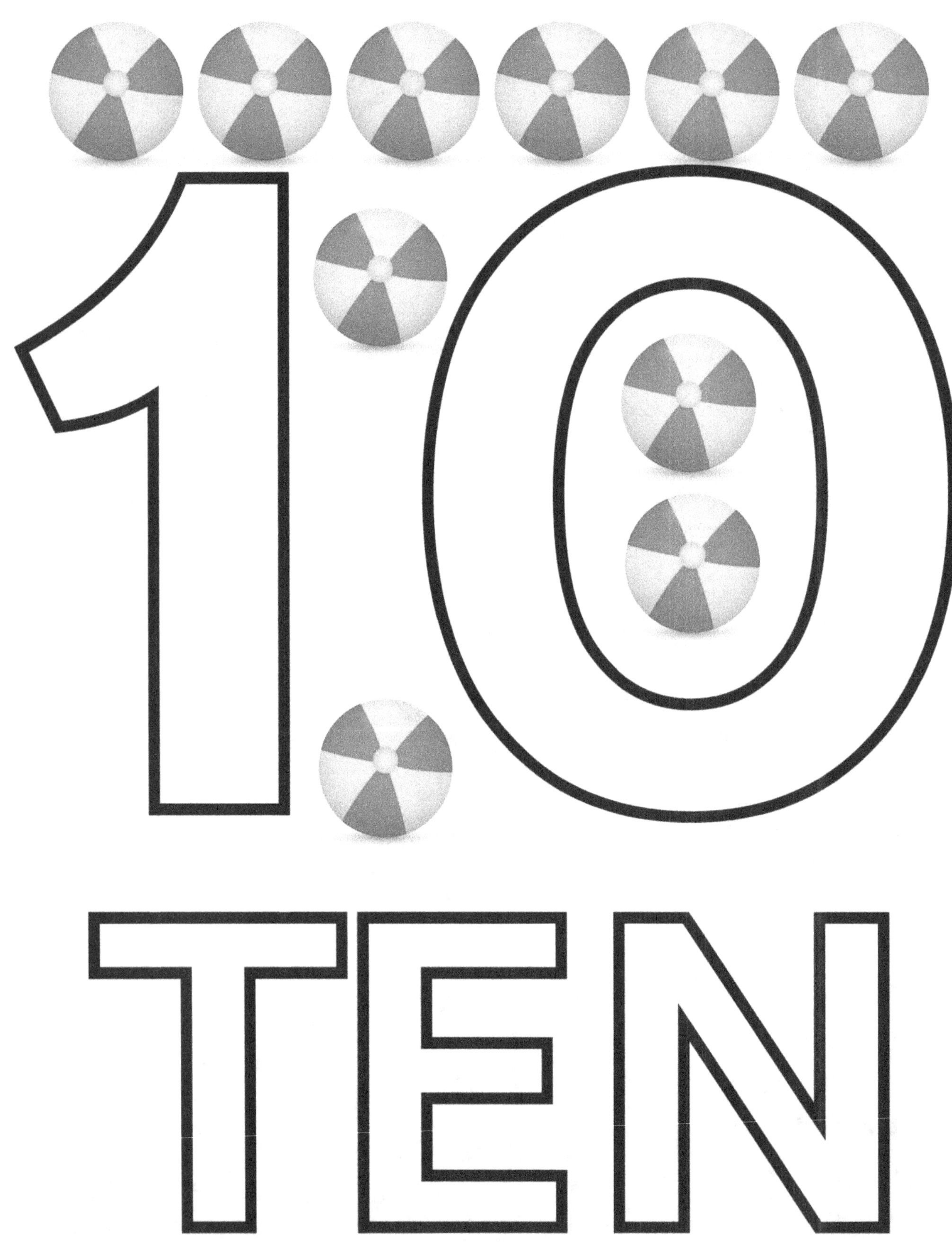

1.0
TEN

Apple
A

B

Banana

C
Coconut

D

Dragon

Elderberry

F

Guava

H
Huckleberry

I ce
Cream

Jujuba
J

K

Kiwi

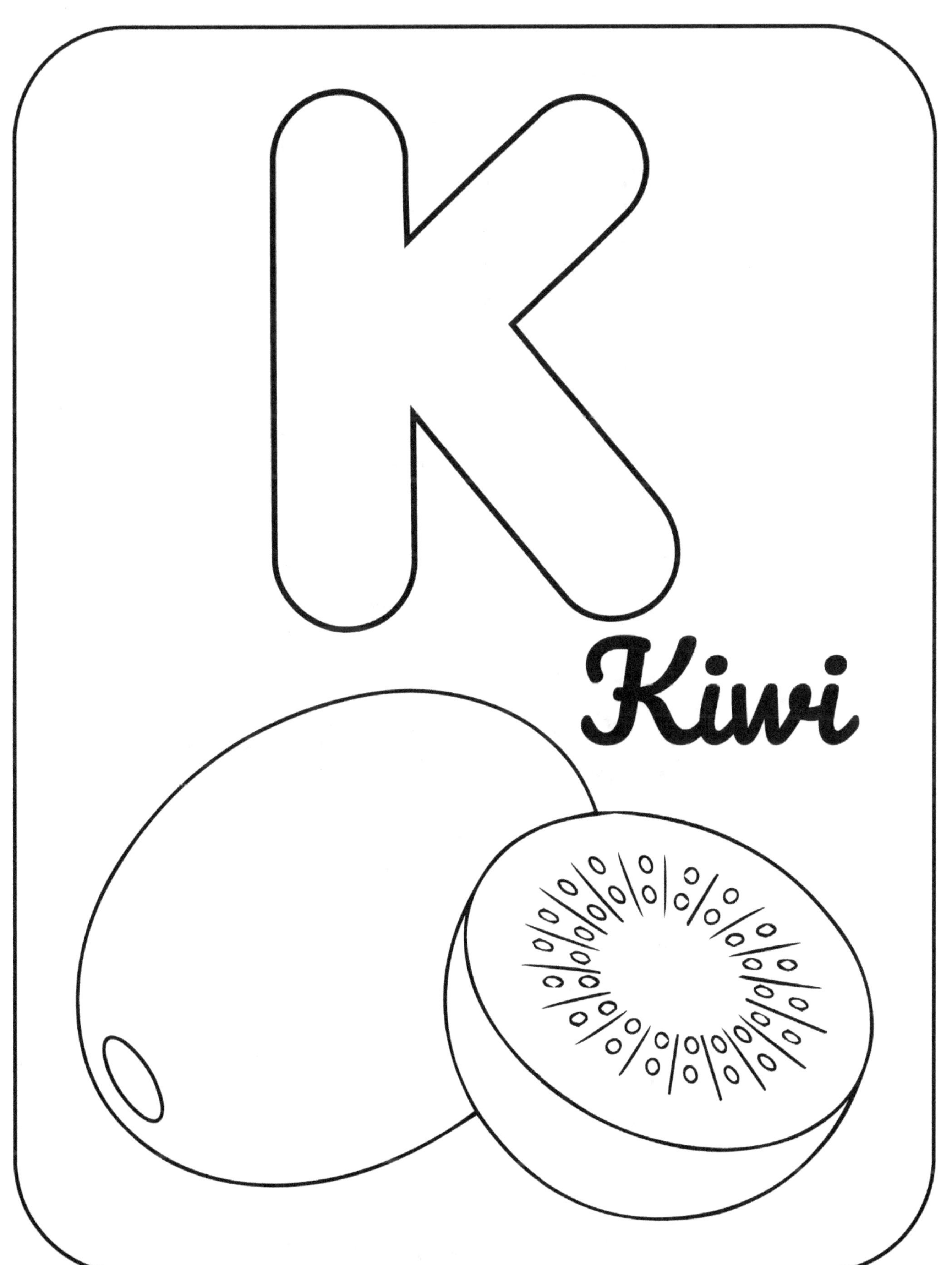

L
Lemon

M
Mango

N

Nectarine

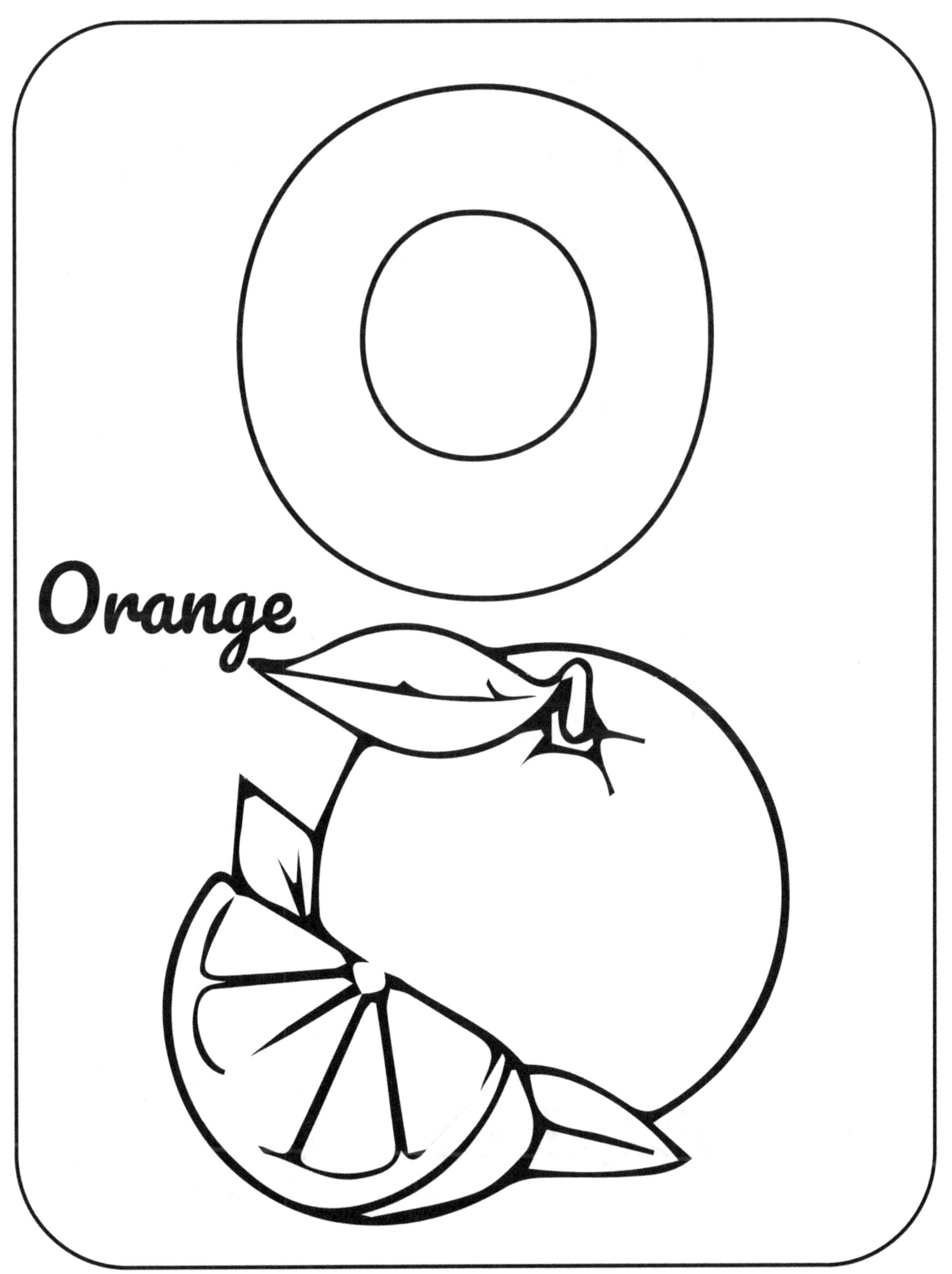

Orange

Pineapple

Q

Quince

R

Radish

S
Strawberry

T
Tomato

Ugly Fruit

V
Vidalia Onions

W
Watermelon

X
Ximenia

Y
Yam

Z
Zucchini

1 2 3 4
5 6 7 8
9 10
NUMBER

1

ONE

2
TWO

4
FOUR

5

FIVE

6
SIX

7

SEVEN

EIGHT

9
NINE

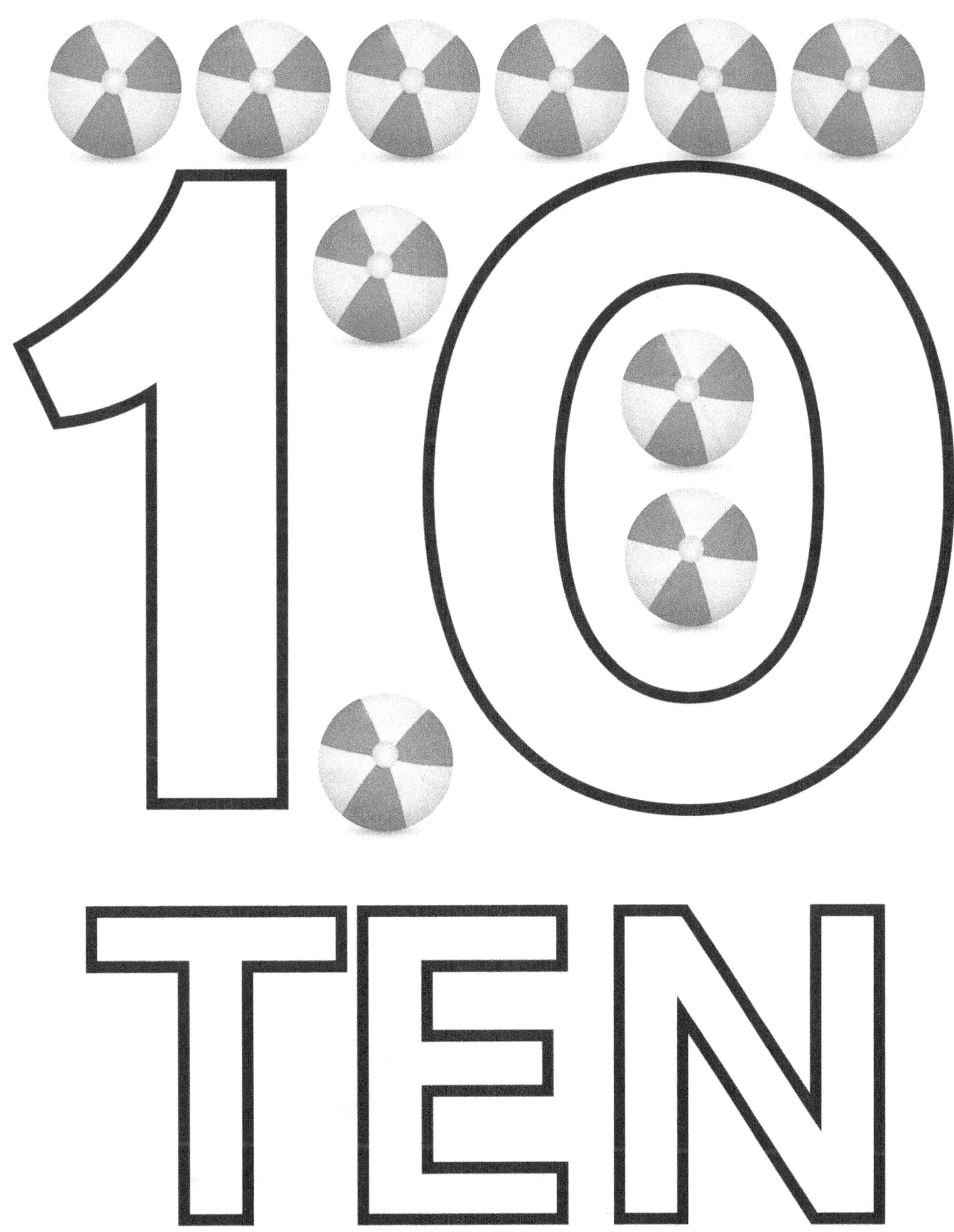

10
TEN

Apple

Banana

Coconut

D

Dragon

E
Elderberry

F
Feijoa

G
Guava

H
Huckleberry

I ce   Cream

Jujuba
J

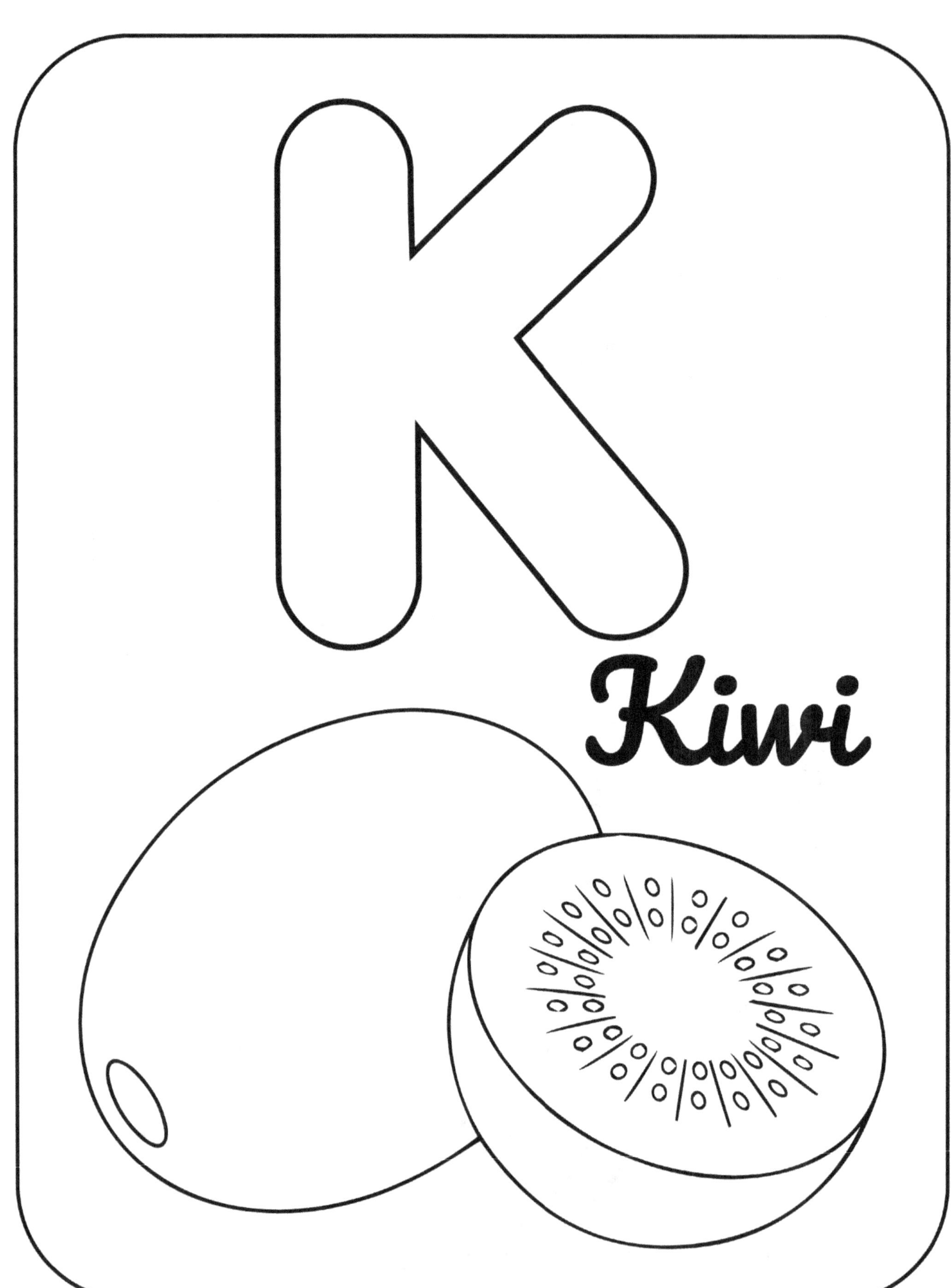

K
Kiwi

Lemon

M
Mango

N

Nectarine

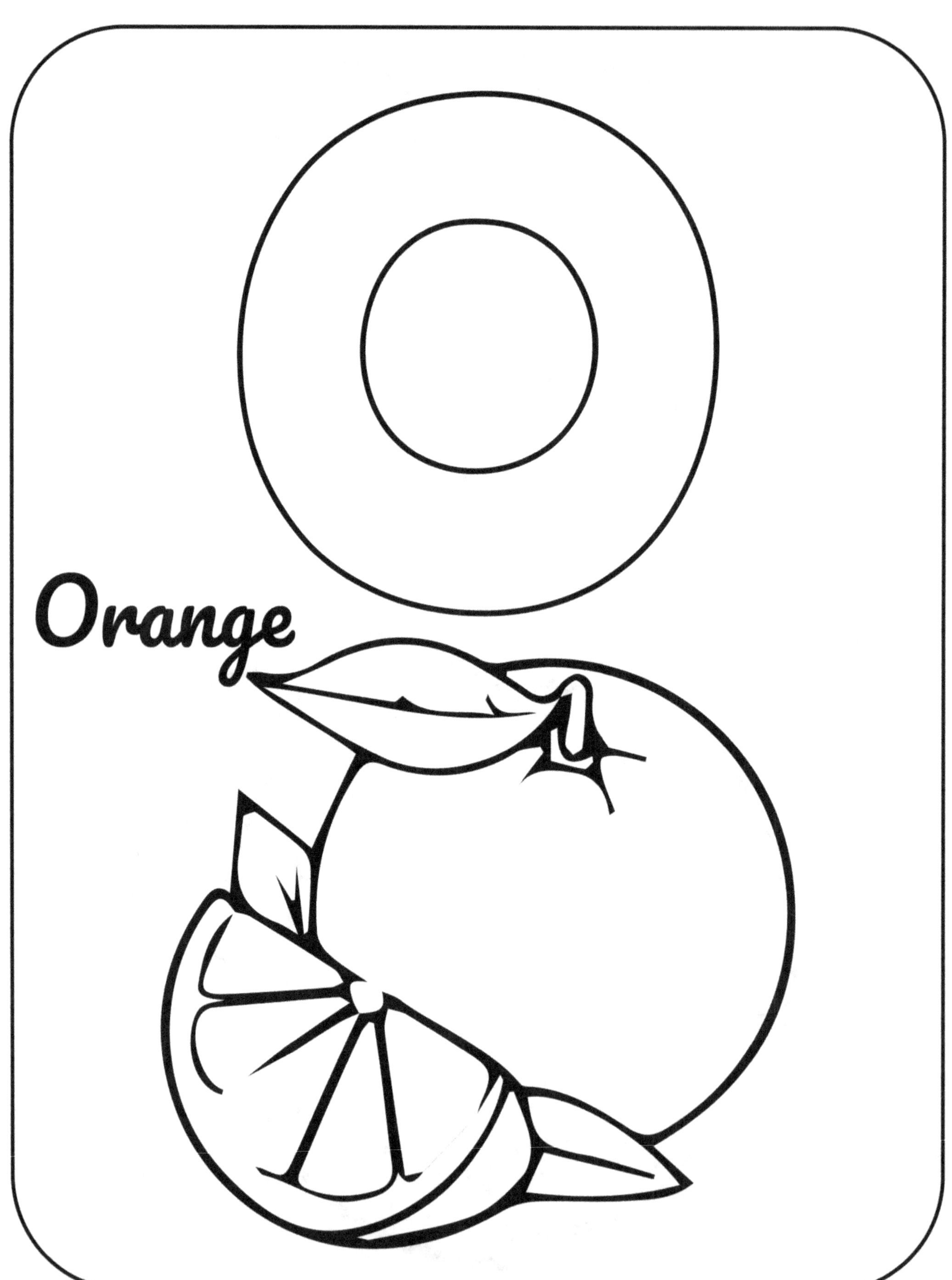

Orange

Pineapple

Quince

R
Radish

S
Strawberry

T
Tomato

Ugly Fruit

V
Vidalia Onions

W
Watermelon

Ximenia

Y
Yam

Z

Zucchini

1 2 3 4
5 6 7 8
9 10
NUMBER

ONE

2

THREE

4
FOUR

5
FIVE

6
SIX

SEVEN

EIGHT

9
NINE

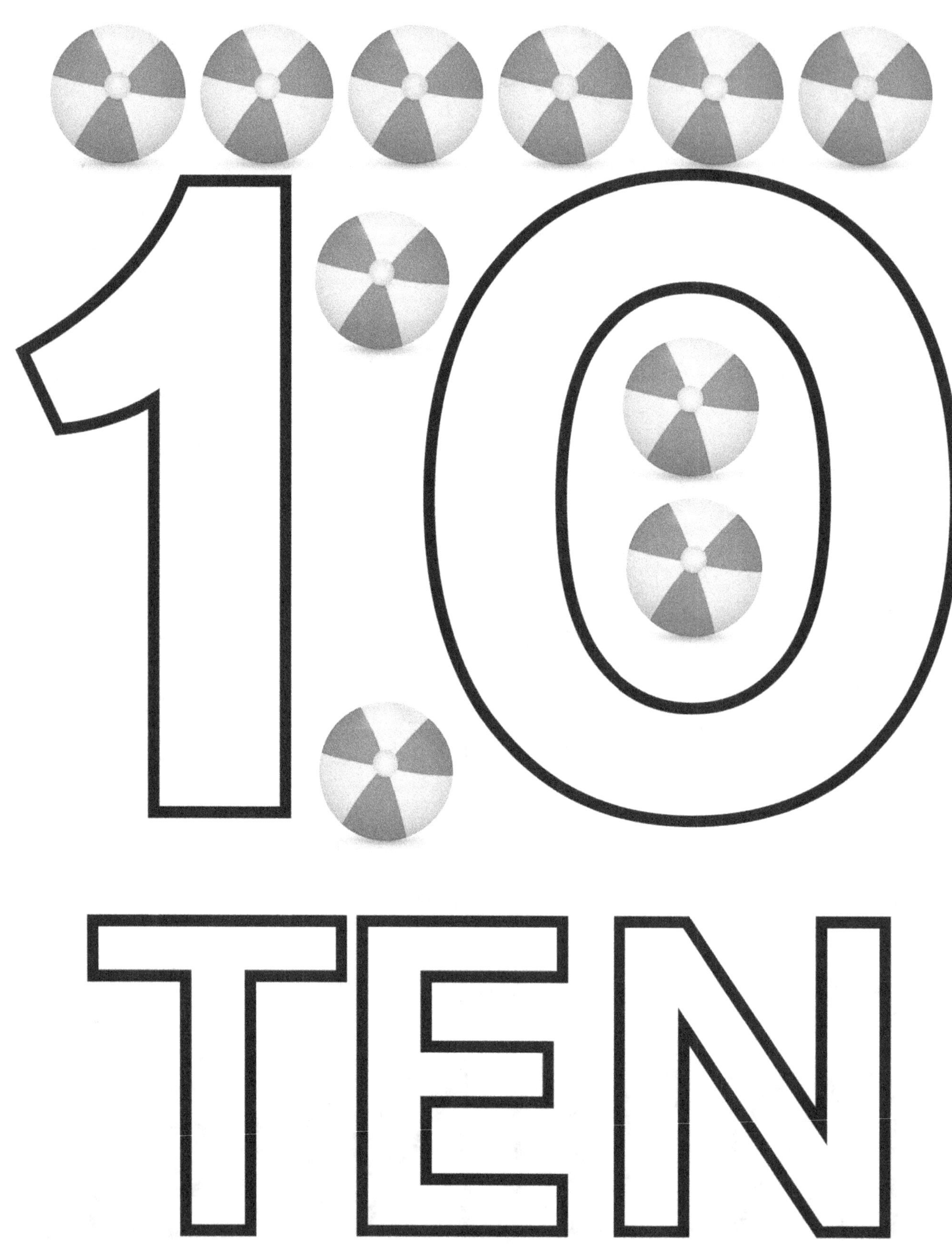

Apple
A

B

Banana

C
Coconut

D

Dragon

Elderberry

F
Feijoa

Guava

Huckleberry

www.ingramcontent.com/pod-product-compliance
Lightning Source LLC
Chambersburg PA
CBHW082340270726
48658CB00017B/2916